Spelling

GRADE 2

Editor
Eric Migliaccio

Managing Editor
Ina Massler Levin, M.A.

Editor-in-Chief
Sharon Coan, M.S. Ed.

Illustrator
Sue Fullam

Cover Artist
Janet Chadwick

Art Coordinator
Kevin Barnes

Art Director
CJae Froshay

Imaging
Rosa C. See

Product Manager
Phil Garcia

Publishers
Rachelle Cracchiolo, M.S. Ed.
Mary Dupuy Smith, M.S. Ed.

Author

Debra J. Housel, M.S. Ed.

Teacher Created Materials, Inc.
6421 Industry Way
Westminster, CA 92683
www.teachercreated.com
ISBN-0-7439-3772-X
©2003 Teacher Created Materials, Inc.
Reprinted, 2003
Made in U.S.A.

Table of Contents

Introduction

The old adage "practice makes perfect" can really hold true for your child's education. The more practice and exposure your child has with concepts being taught in school, the more success he or she is likely to find. For many parents, knowing how to help their child may be frustrating because the resources may not be readily available. As a parent, it is also difficult to know where to focus your efforts so that the extra practice your child receives at home supports what he or she is learning in school.

This book has been written to help parents and teachers reinforce basic skills with children. *Practice Makes Perfect: Spelling* covers basic spelling skills for second graders. The exercises in this book can be completed in any order. The practice included in this book will meet or reinforce educational standards and objectives similar to the ones required by your state and school district for second graders:

- The student will recognize the spelling patterns for short and long vowel sounds.

- The student will know the most common digraphs' sounds and spellings.

- The student will understand r-controlled vowels.

- The student will know when the letter "y" is functioning as a consonant and when it acts as a vowel.

- The student will spell high-frequency words, the 1,000 words that make up 90 percent of all written material. The majority of the words in these spelling lessons are these high-frequency words.

- The student will use a knowledge of word patterns (also called word families) to figure out how to spell and decode new words.

How to Make the Most of This Book

Here are some ideas for making the most of this book:

- Set aside a specific place in your home to work on this book. Keep it neat and tidy, with the necessary materials on hand.

- Determine a specific time of day to work on these practice pages to establish consistency. Look for times in your day or week that are less hectic and more conducive to practicing skills.

- Keep all practice sessions with your child positive and constructive. If your child becomes frustrated or tense, do not force your child to perform. Set the book aside and try again another time.

- Review and praise the work your child has done.

- Allow the child to use whatever writing instrument he or she prefers. For example, colored pencils add variety and pleasure to drill work.

- Introduce the spelling words in the list. Discuss how the words are different and how they are alike. Read the "In Context" column together. Be sure that the students understand the meaning of each word. Stress how words that are spelled alike often rhyme.

- Assist young readers in understanding directions and decoding sentences.

- If time permits, do the additional practice suggestion given for each lesson.

"Y" at the Beginning

The letter "y" is a consonant at the beginning of a word.

Words	In Context
yes	Did Dad say **yes** or no?
yet	The mail has not come **yet**.
you	I think **you** are very nice!
your	Is that **your** coat over there?
young	The **young** bird could not fly.
yard	I found it in our **yard**.
year	Next **year** you will be in third grade.
you're (*you are*)	Cindy, **you're** my best friend.
yellow	I like the color **yellow** the best.
yourself	Can you read the book to **yourself**?

Is the **dark word** spelled wrong in the sentences below? If it is wrong, draw a line under it. If it is right, circle **OK**.

1. He is in the back **yerd**.   OK

2. Did **you** find the book?   OK

3. The teacher looks **yung**.   OK

4. Tim said **yes** when asked if he wanted ice cream.   OK

5. Is this **yor** toy?   OK

6. This **year** I will plant a tree.   OK

7. He is not here **yet**.   OK

8. You look great in that **yello** dress.   OK

9. I think that **you're** unhappy.   OK

10. Did you **yourselve** make sure the door was shut?   OK

- -

Ask your child to write the spelling words in sentences, allowing him or her to draw any parts of the sentence he or she chooses (except for the spelling word). For example: The 🐢 is young.

Y at the Beginning

Word Sort

Write each spelling word in the correct box. Remember "y" is a consonant as the first letter of a word.

Has 2 Consonants

_____

_____

_____

_____

Has 3 Consonants

_____

_____

Has 4 Consonants

_____

Write the word that has only one consonant: _____

Write the word that has five consonants: _____

"Y" at the End Says Long "e"

The letter "y" can act as a vowel. At the end of a word, "y" usually says long "e."

Words	In Context
any	I did not eat **any** cake.
many	We saw **many** flowers.
very	It was a **very** big box.
pretty	The **pretty** girl smiled at me.
only	Sue needs **only** 20 cents more to purchase lunch.
study	He needs to **study** math.
every	Our teacher gives us homework **every** week.
story	Please tell us a **story**.
city	She lives in a large **city**.
happy	They were **happy** when the rain stopped.

Choose the word that best completes each sentence below. Write it on the line.

1. We plan to go to the _____ tomorrow. (**sity, city**)

2. You can set that box on _____ table. (**any, aney**)

3. Tess was _____ beautiful. (**viry, very**)

4. The new rug was quite _____. (**pretty, pritty**)

5. I will be _____ to help you. (**happy, hapy**)

6. Tom has looked in _____ place, but he can't find it. (**every, evere**)

7. They have _____ one child. (**onely, only**)

8. Please tell me a _____. (**storey, story**)

9. If you do not _____, you may fail the test. (**study, studey**)

10. How _____ more boxes do you need? (**meny, many**)

Write each spelling word three times: once in pencil, once with colored pencil, and once with marking pen.

"Y" at the End Says Long "e"

Smiley Faces

Write the first letter of each word in the left eye. Write the last letter of each word in the right eye. Write the whole word as a smile. Here is an example:

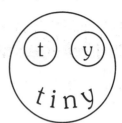

"Y" at the End Says Long "i"

The letter "y" can act as a vowel. At the end of a word, "y" usually says long "e."
But in a few words, "y" says long "i."

Words	In Context
by	He sat **by** the door.
my	Do you think that **my** dress is pretty?
try	She will **try** to fix the broken pot.
fry	My dad can **fry** the meat.
dry	You need some **dry** clothes.
fly	The plane will **fly** high.
sky	The **sky** was blue.
why	I want to know **why** you left.
reply	When I asked him, he did not **reply**.
supply	The school has a **supply** of paper.

Copy the words in the first column. Then, number them in order from A–Z. You
may need to look at the second letter. Next, write the words in A–Z order.

Word	Number	A-Z Order (1-10)
1.		
2.		
3.		
4.		
5.		
6.		
7.		
8.		
9.		
10.		

Make some chocolate pudding (or another flavor with color) and let
your child use craft sticks to "write" the words in pudding in Z-A order
on large, sturdy pieces of heavy paper or cardboard.

"Y" at the End Says Long "i"

Rainbow Words

Which two words have *more* than 3 letters? Write them here:

_____   _____

Write the rest of the words in the bands of the rainbows.
Then, color the rainbows.

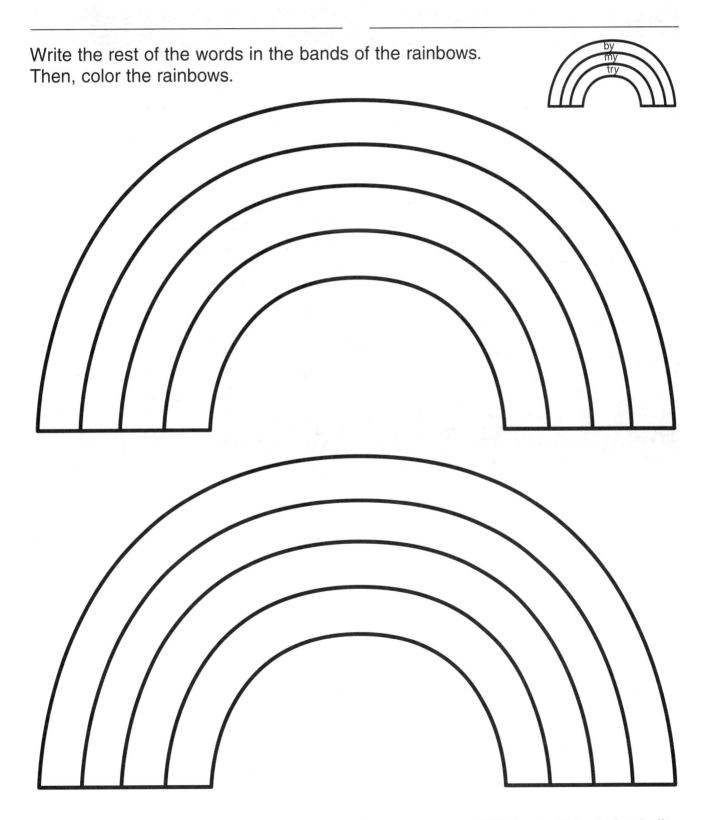

Ending "e" Spelling Pattern: "ake"

When letters form this pattern—vowel, consonant, and the letter "e"—the vowel says its name. The "e" says nothing. In these words, the "a" says its name. The "e" is quiet.

Words	In Context
make	He will **make** a kite.
take	Don't **take** the last piece of pie.
lake	Let's go swim in the **lake**.
cake	She made a white **cake**.
rake	We will **rake** the leaves.
bake	They want to **bake** cookies.
brake	To stop the car, press the **brake**.
fake	A wig is made of **fake** hair.
sake	For my dog's **sake**, I buy the best dog food.
shake	Please **shake** the dirt out of this rug.

Copy the spelling words in the first column. If you can add "d" to make a real word, write it in the second column. If you can add "s" to make a real word, write it in the third column.

Spelling Word	Does adding "d" to the end make a *real* world?	Does adding "s" to the end make a *real* world?
ex. snake	NO	snakes
1.		
2.		
3.		
4.		
5.		
6.		
7.		
8.		
9.		
10.		

Spray shaving cream on a desktop or on a cookie sheet. Have the child trace each spelling word in the shaving cream.

Ending "e" Spelling Pattern: "ake"

Word Pyramids

Write each word inside the pyramid. Follow this format:

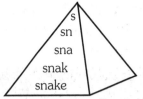

Ending "e" Spelling Pattern: "ame"

When letters form this pattern—vowel, consonant, and the letter "e"—the vowel says its name. The "e" says nothing. In these words, the "a" says it name. The "e" is quiet.

Words	In Context
name	What is your **name**?
same	The two cards look just the **same**.
came	She **came** late to the party.
game	Let's play a **game**.
tame	That deer acts like it's **tame**.
fame	His **fame** spread all over the world.
flame	The candle's **flame** blew out.
frame	I need a new **frame** for this picture.
blame	You cannot **blame** him for being sick.
became	The storm **became** worse as we went east.

Is the **dark word** spelled wrong in the sentences below? If it is wrong, draw a line under it. If it is right, circle **OK**.

1. Do you know how to **tame** a bird?   OK
2. Would you like to play a **gam** with us?   OK
3. His **naim** is Sam.   OK
4. Did he take the **blame** for the torn book?   OK
5. That **frame** looks great on that picture.   OK
6. They **cam** home yesterday.   OK
7. Their music brought them **fame**.   OK
8. Is that book the **same** as this one?   OK
9. The water made the **flime** go out.   OK
10. The lake **bcame** deep just ten feet from the shore. OK

Cut out sandpaper letters. Have your child use the letters to form the words in the list. This way he or she will internalize that the only difference between "came" and "game" is the first letter. It also helps the child to comprehend how "fame" turns into "frame."

Ending "e" Spelling Pattern: "ame"

Word Wagons

Put the first letter in the left wheel. Put the last letter in the right wheel. Write the whole word inside the wagon.

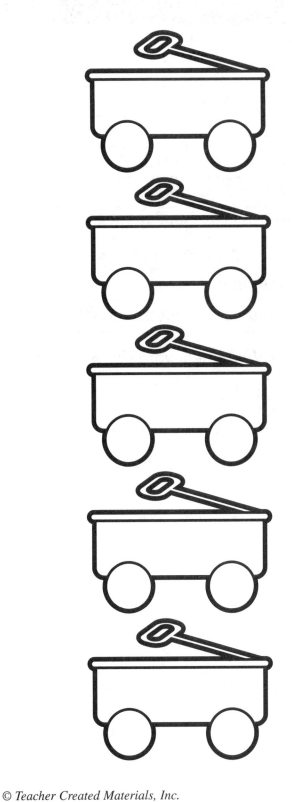

Ending "e" Spelling Pattern: "ide"

When letters form this pattern—vowel, consonant, and the letter "e"—the vowel says its name. The "e" says nothing. In these words, the "i" says its name. The "e" is quiet.

Words	In Context
ride	Do you **ride** a bus to school?
wide	The river was very **wide**.
tide	The **tide** started to come in.
hide	Let's play **hide** and seek.
bride	The **bride** looked pretty at her wedding.
side	This **side** of the box is bright red.
inside	It was so cold that he went back **inside**.
outside	Bring the dog in. Don't leave her **outside**.
beside	The paper was **beside** the front step.
decide	Did you **decide** what you want to eat yet?

Circle the word below that is **not** spelled right. Write each word correctly.

1. inside   insied   _____
2. bried   bride   _____
3. beside   besside   _____
4. wide   wied   _____
5. deside   decide   _____
6. teid   tide   _____
7. side   seid   _____
8. ried   ride   _____
9. outside   ootside   _____
10. hyde   hide   _____

- -

Ask your child to write the spelling words, then underline each vowel and circle each consonant.

Ending "e" Spelling Pattern: "ide"

Word Study

Copy each spelling word. Count the consonants in each word. Count the vowels in each word.

Spelling Word	Consonants	Vowels
1.		
2.		
3.		
4.		
5.		
6.		
7.		
8.		
9.		
10.		

11. Which word has the most vowels? _____

bride

tide

Ending "e" Spelling Pattern: "oke"

When letters form this pattern—vowel, consonant, and the letter "e"—the vowel says its name. The "e" says nothing. In these words, the "o" says its name. The "e" is quiet.

Words	In Context
joke	Isn't that a funny **joke**?
poke	Do not **poke** your brother!
spoke	She **spoke** so softly. We couldn't hear her.
smoke	The **smoke** was thick and black.
stoke	Would you please **stoke** the fire?
broke	The lamp **broke** when it fell off the table.
woke	They **woke** up.
awoke	We **awoke** at 7 a.m.
choke	He began to **choke** on the hot dog.
stroke	I like to **stroke** my pet's head.

Choose the word below that best completes the sentence. Write it on the line.

1. I _____ with her yesterday. (**spoke, spoak**)

2. The cat likes it when you _____ her back. (**stroek, stroke**)

3. Don't put so much in your mouth! You could _____. (**choke, choak**)

4. Jen adds logs to _____ the fire. (**stoke, stook**)

5. Gina _____ a plate. (**brook, broke**)

6. Oh, no! I _____ up too late! (**woak, woke**)

7. Thick _____ rose from the fire. (**smoke, smoek**)

8. Did you get my _____? (**joke, joak**)

9. Do not _____ the puppy when he's asleep! (**pook, poke**)

10. The baby _____ due to all the noise. (**awoke, awoek**)

Write each spelling word once in lowercase letters and once using all uppercase letters.

Ending "E" Spelling Pattern: "oke"

Barbells

Write the first letter of each word in the left circle. Write the last letter of each word in the right circle. Write the rest of the word in between, like this:

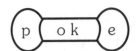

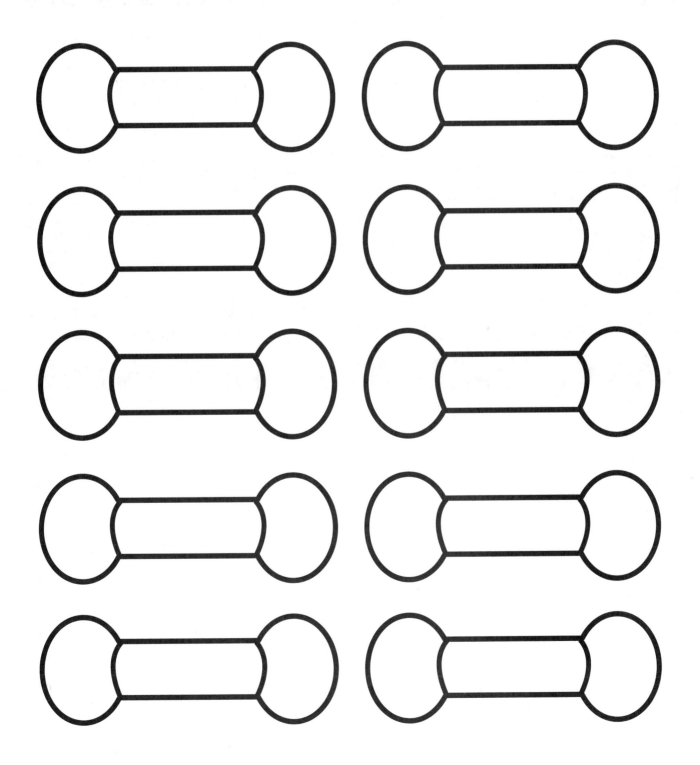

Two Vowels Together: "ay"

The letter "y" can act as a vowel. When two vowels stand together, as in "ay," the first one says its name. The second one is silent.

Words	In Context
way	Please move those boxes out of my **way**.
day	It was a bright, sunny **day**.
may	He **may** stay home this afternoon.
say	I don't know what she will **say**.
stay	Ben will **stay** there.
lay	Please **lay** the papers on the table.
pay	Do you have the money to **pay** for it?
play	She likes to **play** with me.
away	We don't want to move **away**.
always	You **always** cheer me up.

Copy the words in the first column. Number them in order from A–Z. You may need to look at the second letter. Next, write the words in A–Z order.

	Word	Number	A-Z Order (1–10)
1.			
2.			
3.			
4.			
5.			
6.			
7.			
8.			
9.			
10.			

Allow your child to dictate a story to you, being certain to use all of the spelling words (in any order) at least once. Record the story and reread it together.

Two Vowels Together: "ay"

Word Web

Write the letters "ay" in the center of the web. Write the two
words that begin with "a" on the lines under the web.
Write the other eight words on the strands of the web.

_____   _____

Two Vowels Together: "ain"

The letters "a" and "i" are both vowels. When two vowels stand together, the first one says its name. The second one is silent. The letters "ain" form a spelling pattern.

Words	In Context
rain	It began to **rain**.
main	Their act is the **main** one.
train	What time is your **train**?
gain	You need to **gain** a few more pounds.
stain	She got a **stain** on her skirt.
chain	He had a gold **chain** around his neck.
plain	His room was not fancy. It was **plain**.
explain	Please **explain** how to do it.
remain	Our cat will **remain** in the house while we are out.
contain	What does the box **contain**?

Is the **dark word** spelled wrong in the sentence below? If it is wrong, draw a line under it. If it is right, circle **OK**.

1. The **rain** stopped.   OK
2. Can you **explane** how to get there?   OK
3. We are going by **train**.   OK
4. She is the **mian** person in charge here.   OK
5. The rug had a bad **stain**.   OK
6. Her dress was quite **plain**.   OK
7. Did you **gian** weight?   OK
8. Your kit will **cuntain** all of the parts.   OK
9. The dog was on a long **chane**.   OK
10. Please **remain** in your seats.   OK

- -

Make a chart with these headings: **Word, Vowels, Consonants.** Have the child analyze each word, then fill in the number of vowels and consonants in the appropriate column.

Two Vowels Together: "ain"

Sailboats

Write each word inside the sailboat, like this:

Two Vowels Together: "ail"

The letters "a" and "i" are both vowels. When two vowels stand together, the first one says its name. The second one is silent. The letters "ail" form a spelling pattern.

Words	In Context
sail	We want to **sail** our boats in the pond.
tail	My dog hurt his **tail**.
mail	Please bring in the **mail**.
fail	If I **fail** the test, I will have to take it again.
nail	Hit the **nail** with that hammer.
pail	She will fill this **pail** with water.
hail	Bits of **hail** as big as dimes fell from the sky.
rail	You don't want to slip. Hold onto the **rail**.
wail	The baby began to **wail**.
detail	Can you tell me another **detail** about the car?

Copy the spelling words. Write the vowel as an equation. Write the spelling word again.

Spelling Word	Equation	Spelling Word
ex. trail	a + i = long a	trail
1.		
2.		
3.		
4.		
5.		
6.		
7.		
8.		
9.		
10.		

- -

Cut out sandpaper letters. Have your child use the letters to form the words in the list. This way he or she will internalize that the only difference between "fail" and "tail" is the first letter. It also helps the child to comprehend how "tail" turns into "detail."

Two Vowels Together: "ail"

Word Tree

Many words "grow" from the word "ail." Write the longest word under the tree.
Write "ail" on the tree trunk. Write the rest of the words in its branches.

Longest word: _____

Two Vowels Together: "ee"

When two vowels stand together, the first one says its name. The second one is silent. The first "e" says its name and the second "e" is silent.

Words	In Context
need	Will I **need** a hat?
seed	She will plant the flower **seed**.
week	In one **week** we will go to the beach.
seen	They have **seen** my doll.
green	The pine trees were **green**.
feel	Don't **feel** bad. We can fix it.
wheel	His dad fixed the broken **wheel**.
feet	Those shoes hurt my **feet**.
meet	Would you like to **meet** my sister?
street	Turn down the third **street** on the right.

Copy each spelling word. Write the words again, putting the double "e" in a different color. Then write the words one last time, leaving space around the double "e". Circle the double "e".

Word	Write double "e" in a different color	Circle the double "e"
1.		
2.		
3.		
4.		
5.		
6.		
7.		
8.		
9.		
10.		

Write a sentence for each spelling word, including a plural noun (more than one person, place, or thing).

Here is an example: The keys were lost for one week.

Two Vowels Together: "ee"

Word Triangles

Write each spelling word three times to form a triangle, like this:

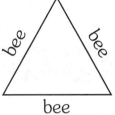

Two Vowels Together: "eep"

When two vowels stand together, the first one says its name. The second one is silent. The letters "eep" form a spelling pattern.

Words	In Context
keep	Please **keep** this ring in a safe place.
deep	The water does not look too **deep**.
sleep	You **sleep** in a bed.
asleep	Shh! My dad is **asleep**.
jeep	My mom got a new **jeep**.
weep	Please do not **weep**.
beep	The car's horn went "**beep**."
sheep	Most **sheep** have white wool.
sweep	Would you **sweep** the floor for me?
steep	The hill was quite **steep**.

Copy each spelling word. Count the consonants in each word. Count the vowels in each word.

	Spelling Word	Consonants	Vowels
1.			
2.			
3.			
4.			
5.			
6.			
7.			
8.			
9.			
10.			

11. Which word has the most vowels? _____

- -

Work with your child to compose a rhyming poem or song using the words in the spelling list.

Two Vowels Together: "eep" *(cont.)*

Word Gates

Put the first letter in the left post. Put the last letter in the right post. Write the whole word on the door of the gate.

creep

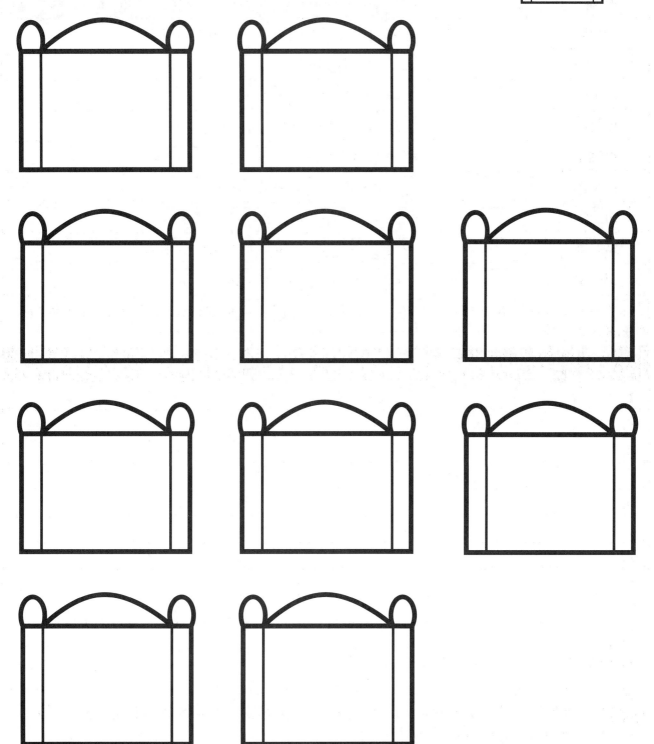

Two Vowels Together: "ea"

The letters "e" and "a" are both vowels. When two vowels stand together, the first one says its name. The second one is silent. The letters "ea" form a spelling pattern.

Words	In Context
easy	It might be **easy** to do.
please	Will you **please** stop doing that!
sea	Their house is near the **sea**.
real	Is the gem in that ring **real**?
deal	My brother got a good **deal** on that car.
mean	His cat is **mean**.
clean	Keep your room neat and **clean**.
speaks	She **speaks** too softly.
team	I hope our **team** wins this game.
east	The sun always rises in the **east**.

Below, draw a line to match the words that rhyme.

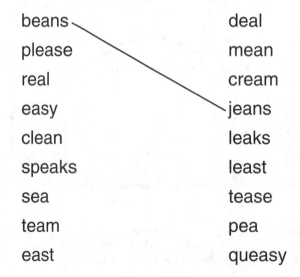

beans	deal
please	mean
real	cream
easy	jeans
clean	leaks
speaks	least
sea	tease
team	pea
east	queasy

Have the child use each spelling word in an oral sentence or question spoken to an adult. Spell out the words in the list. For example: "East: The sun rises in the e-a-s-t.".

Two Vowels Together: "ea"

Word Web

Write the letters "ea" in the center of the web. Write the two longest words on the lines under the web. Write the eight other words on the strands of the web.

Two Vowels Together: "eat"

The letters "e" and "a" are both vowels. When two vowels stand together, the first one says its name. The second one is silent. The letters "eat" form a spelling pattern.

Words	In Context
eat	We **eat** lunch at noon.
beat	I **beat** him in a race.
heat	Mom will **heat** the meal.
meat	We ate **meat** and rice.
seat	He found a **seat** near the steps.
neat	Keep your things **neat**.
treat	My dog loves to get a **treat**.
cheat	Do not **cheat** to win the game.
wheat	Bread is made from **wheat**.
repeat	Can you **repeat** what you just said?

Copy the words in the first column. Number them in order from A–Z. Next, write the words in A–Z order.

	Word	Number	A-Z Order (1–10)
1.			
2.			
3.			
4.			
5.			
6.			
7.			
8.			
9.			
10.			

Have your child dictate to you a sentence or a question for each spelling word that includes a cartoon character, fairy tale character, or super hero's name as the subject. Record the sentences, then ask the child to highlight the spelling word.

Two Vowels Together: "eat"

Word Tree

Many words "grow" from the word "eat." Write the longest word under the tree. Write "eat" on the tree trunk. Write the rest of the words in its branches.

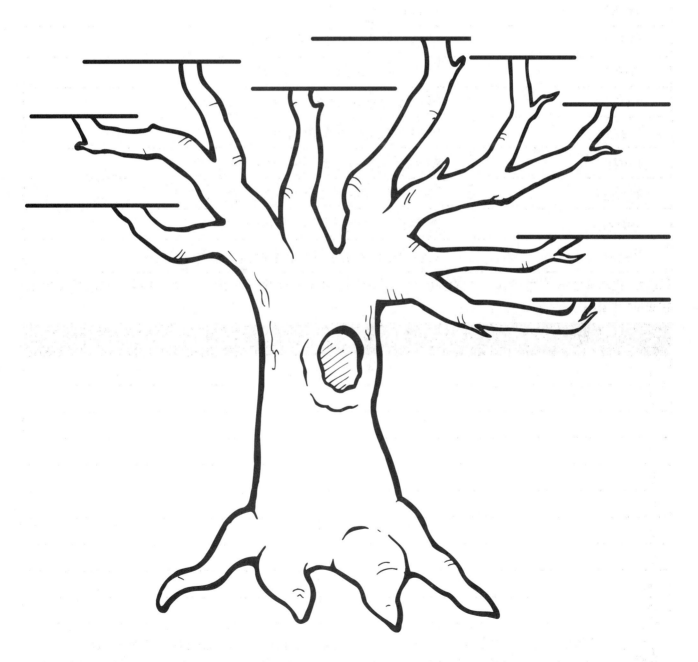

Longest word: _____

Two Vowels Together: "oa"

The letters "o" and "a" are both vowels. When two vowels stand together, the first one says its name. The second one is silent. Look for the "oa" in each of these words:

Words	In Context
road	Do you live on this **road**?
toad	The **toad** sat in the sun.
load	He had a big **load** to carry.
boat	I saw a big **boat** on the lake.
coat	Where is my **coat**?
goat	Let me pet the **goat**.
float	Will it **float** in water?
soak	The rice must **soak** before we eat it.
goal	She made a soccer **goal**.
coast	The storm moved along the sea **coast**.

Copy each spelling word. Write the vowel as an equation. Write the spelling word again.

Spelling Word	Equation	Spelling Word
ex. oak	o + a = long o	oak
1.		
2.		
3.		
4.		
5.		
6.		
7.		
8.		
9.		
10.		

Have your child write the spelling words in reverse alphabetical order, Z–A.

Two Vowels Together: "oa"

Word Triangles

Write each spelling word three times to form a triangle, like this:

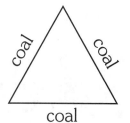

Two Vowels Together: "ui" & "ue"

The letters "u," "e," and "i" are all vowels. When two vowels stand together, the first one says its name. The second one is silent. The vowels "ui" and "ue" say the long "u" sound. Look for "ui" or "ue" in each of these words:

Words	In Context
fruit	The kind of **fruit** she likes best is oranges.
suit	You look great in that **suit**!
ruin	Water will **ruin** the paper.
due	This book is **due** next week.
blue	He has on a **blue** shirt.
true	Is it **true** that you are moving?
clue	Can you tell me a **clue** about my gift?
argue	Let's not **argue** about it.
value	That stamp is old and has great **value**.
continue	We will **continue** to go down this road.

Choose the word that best completes each sentence. Write it on the line.

1. Let's _____ until we see a rest stop. (**continu**, **continue**)

2. Do not add salt. It will _____ the candy. (**riun**, **ruin**)

3. We could not walk far _____ to the deep snow. (**due**, **du**)

4. The sky is so _____ today! (**blu**, **blue**)

5. An apple is a kind of _____. (**fruit**, **frute**)

6. They _____ always telling the truth. (**valu**, **value**)

7. If it is not false, then it is _____. (**true**, **treu**)

8. Did you get a new _____? (**sute**, **suit**)

9. I need a _____ to find out where my dog went. (**klue**, **clue**)

10. Let's not _____ over the last piece of pie. (**argue**, **ageru**)

- -

Write each spelling word three times in a row. Circle or highlight the best handwriting for each word.

Two Vowels Together: "ui" & "ue"

Word Study

Copy each spelling word. Count the consonants in each word. Count the vowels in each word.

Spelling Word	Consonants	Vowels
1.		
2.		
3.		
4.		
5.		
6.		
7.		
8.		
9.		
10.		

11. Which word has the most vowels? _____

Loud "r": "ar"

The letter "r" is loud. It shouts over the top of any vowel that is in front of it. So when a vowel is followed by "r," you hear the loud "r" instead of the vowel.

Words	In Context
large	The **large** bear moved slowly.
start	When did you **start** learning to ride a bike?
hard	It was **hard** not to slip and fall.
car	The **car** broke down.
far	We do not want to move **far** away.
arm	She hurt her **arm** yesterday.
farm	I used to live on a **farm**.
mark	Use that pen to **mark** the paper.
dark	It was a **dark**, rainy night.
party	Are you coming to my **party**?

Draw a line to match the words that rhyme.

1. yarn   barge

2. hard   far

3. arm   barn

4. mark   smart

5. start   card

6. car   farm

7. large   dark

8. Which spelling word from the list above is not in the matching activity?

_____

Write each spelling word with its matching word next to it. See if you can add another word to make three rhyming words. Here is an example from the lesson: <u>**car**</u>   <u>**far**</u>   <u>**bar**</u>

Loud "r": "ar"

Using a Dictionary.

Guide words are in dark print at the top of each dictionary page. You look at them to see if the word you want falls *between* them.

Copy each spelling word. Look up each one in a dictionary. What are the two guide words at the top of the page? Write the guide words.

Spelling Word	Left-Side Guide Word	Right-Side Guide Word
ex. bark	bare	base
1.		
2.		
3.		
4.		
5.		
6.		
7.		
8.		
9.		
10.		

Loud "r": "er"

The letter "r" is loud. It shouts over the top of any vowel that is in front of it. So when a vowel is followed by "r," you hear the loud "r" instead of the vowel.

Words	In Context
her	Their mother is calling **her**.
water	The **water** was not too deep.
over	Reach up **over** your head.
ever	Do you **ever** find it hard to fall asleep?
never	I **never** want to fail a test.
after	Tuesday comes **after** Monday.
under	He found it **under** the bed.
paper	Put your name on your **paper**.
person	That **person** looks like my dad.
number	What is your phone **number**?

Copy each spelling word. Write the words again, putting the loud "r" and vowels in a different color. Then write the words one last time, leaving space around the loud "r" and vowels. Circle the loud "r" and vowels.

Word	Vowel & loud "r" in different color	Circle vowel & loud "r"
1.		
2.		
3.		
4.		
5.		
6.		
7.		
8.		
9.		
10.		

Write the words in the list in reverse alphabetical order (Z–A).

Loud "r": "er"

Word Sort

Write each spelling word in the correct box. Remember that "r" is a consonant even though it affects the vowel.

Has 2 Consonants

_____

_____

_____

Has 3 Consonants

_____

_____

_____

_____

_____

Has 4 Consonants

_____

_____

Loud "r": "or"

The letter "r" is loud. It shouts over the top of any vowel that is in front of it. So when a vowel is followed by "r," you hear the loud "r" instead of the vowel.

Words	In Context
for	That gift is **for** me.
more	The ducks want to eat **more** corn.
short	She is too **short** to reach that shelf.
form	You must fill out this **form.**
story	Please write a **story**.
horse	The **horse** ran very fast.
born	In what month were you **born**?
corn	Your field of **corn** is growing well.
before	Wednesday comes **before** Thursday.
doctor	My **doctor** helps me when I am ill.

Circle the word that is **not** spelled right. Write each word correctly.

1. mor   more   _____

2. doctor   docter   _____

3. for   fore   _____

4. hoers   horse   _____

5. corn   conr   _____

6. foorm   form   _____

7. boern   born   _____

8. before   befor   _____

9. short   shart   _____

10. storie   story   _____

- -

Write the spelling words. Use color pencil or marker to circle the "r" and the vowel it controls.

Loud "r": "or"

Phone Code

Did you know that phones have numbers
and letters on their keys? Write each word.
Then write the word again using its numbers.

1	2 ABC	3 DEF
4 GHI	5 JKL	6 MNO
7 PRS	8 TUV	9 WXY
*	0	#

Spelling Word	Phone Code for Word
ex. corner	267637
1.	
2.	
3.	
4.	
5.	
6.	
7.	
8.	
9.	
10.	

11. Which two words have the same phone code?

_____ and _____

Loud "r": "ir" and "ur"

The letter "r" is loud. It shouts over the top of any vowel that is in front of it. So when a vowel is followed by "r," you hear the loud "r" instead of the vowel.

Words	In Context
first	Last year you were in **first** grade.
girl	A new **girl** moved in this week.
bird	I could see a **bird** at the feeder.
third	My sister is in **third** grade.
direct	This is the most **direct** path.
sir	Are you ready to order, **sir**? (like Mr.)
circle	He colored the **circle** orange.
burn	The stove gave her a bad **burn**.
turn	Please **turn** off the TV.
return	When will you **return** home?

Is the **dark word** spelled wrong in the sentences below? If it is wrong, draw a line under it. If it is right, circle **OK**.

1. I must **retern** the shirt. It does not fit.   OK

2. How old is that **girl**?   OK

3. Form a **cirkle** around the room.   OK

4. It is Joe's **turn** next.   OK

5. He went to **first** grade last year.   OK

6. The paper began to **burn**.   OK

7. May I help you, **ser**?   OK

8. A **berd** made a nest by my window.   OK

9. After the **diret** hit, the chair fell over.   OK

10. Next year you will be in **third** grade.   OK

- -

Write the spelling words. Then use a highlighter to highlight the "r" and the vowel it controls.

Loud "r": "ir" and "ur"

Sailboats

Write each word inside the sailboat. Follow this format:

```
s
si
sir
sir
```

Assessment #1

Read each sentence. Read all of the answers. Fill in the circle of the word that is spelled right and best completes the sentence.

1. **I will come back next _____.**
   - (a) year
   - (b) yer
   - (c) yeer

2. **The puppy is very _____.**
   - (a) yong
   - (b) young
   - (c) yung

3. **He liked your _____ a lot.**
   - (a) storie
   - (b) storey
   - (c) story

4. **She has _____ CDs.**
   - (a) meny
   - (b) many
   - (c) mene

5. **Tell me _____ you are so late.**
   - (a) why
   - (b) wy
   - (c) whey

6. **The _____ stopped the bus.**
   - (a) broke
   - (b) break
   - (c) brake

7. **Is your bird _____ ?**
   - (a) teem
   - (b) team
   - (c) tame

8. **The tadpole _____ a toad.**
   - (a) becam
   - (b) became
   - (c) become

9. **Brad just cannot _____.**
   - (a) decide
   - (b) deside
   - (c) decid

10. **She started to choke from all of the _____.**
    - (a) smoke
    - (b) smoak
    - (c) smoek

11. **It was sunny when he _____.**
    - (a) awoak
    - (b) ewoke
    - (c) awoke

12. **Let's _____ a card game.**
    - (a) pay
    - (b) play
    - (c) pray

13. **The _____ moved down the track.**
    - (a) train
    - (b) trane
    - (c) traine

14. **The ship set _____.**
    - (a) share
    - (b) sail
    - (c) stall

15. **The crash bent her bike's _____.**
    - (a) wheel
    - (b) whel
    - (c) wheal

Assessment #2

Read each sentence. Read all of the answers. Fill in the circle of the word that is spelled right and best completes the sentence.

1. **The lost child began to _____.**
   - (a) weap
   - (b) wheep
   - (c) weep

2. **Sam will _____ to the man.**
   - (a) speck
   - (b) speak
   - (c) spoke

3. **It will be _____ to do.**
   - (a) ezy
   - (b) esy
   - (c) easy

4. **The farmer grew _____.**
   - (a) wheat
   - (b) what
   - (c) whet

5. **Where is my black _____?**
   - (a) cite
   - (b) cot
   - (c) coat

6. **The heat may _____ the film.**
   - (a) run
   - (b) ruin
   - (c) ruine

7. **They began to _____.**
   - (a) argu
   - (b) argue
   - (c) arguie

8. **Sue had a _____ yesterday.**
   - (a) partee
   - (b) parte
   - (c) party

9. **Please give me some _____.**
   - (a) water
   - (b) watar
   - (c) watir

10. **We need _____ light over here.**
    - (a) more
    - (b) moor
    - (c) mor

11. **Can you draw a nice, round _____?**
    - (a) airckle
    - (b) circle
    - (c) sirkle

12. **Do you plan to _____ to the park tomorrow?**
    - (a) retern
    - (b) rturn
    - (c) return

13. **Your drawing is quite _____.**
    - (a) prity
    - (b) pretty
    - (c) pritty

14. **He baked a _____ for her birthday.**
    - (a) kake
    - (b) cake
    - (c) cack

15. **If you're not inside, you must be _____.**
    - (a) outside
    - (b) otside
    - (c) outsid

Assessment #3

Read the dark word. Fill in the circle of the word that rhymes with the dark word.

1. **yard**
   - (a) card
   - (b) dark
   - (c) cord

2. **my**
   - (a) shy
   - (b) she
   - (c) slay

3. **bake**
   - (a) cane
   - (b) same
   - (c) quake

4. **frame**
   - (a) lake
   - (b) shame
   - (c) dream

5. **bride**
   - (a) stride
   - (b) need
   - (c) time

6. **joke**
   - (a) dome
   - (b) dock
   - (c) bloke

7. **day**
   - (a) try
   - (b) stray
   - (c) key

8. **chain**
   - (a) grain
   - (b) laid
   - (c) aim

9. **mail**
   - (a) deal
   - (b) frail
   - (c) aid

10. **week**
    - (a) seem
    - (b) deck
    - (c) peek

11. **street**
    - (a) teen
    - (b) sheet
    - (c) greed

12. **jeep**
    - (a) meet
    - (b) keen
    - (c) creep

13. **cheat**
    - (a) beat
    - (b) crate
    - (c) wet

14. **deal**
    - (a) pal
    - (b) fell
    - (c) steal

15. **goal**
    - (a) toad
    - (b) soak
    - (c) foal

16. **true**
    - (a) suit
    - (b) glue
    - (c) cute

17. **start**
    - (a) smart
    - (b) mark
    - (c) port

18. **number**
    - (a) paper
    - (b) labor
    - (c) lumber

19. **form**
    - (a) cord
    - (b) sort
    - (c) storm

20. **girl**
    - (a) skirt
    - (b) swirl
    - (c) still

Answer Key

page 4
1. yard
2. OK
3. young
4. OK
5. your
6. OK
7. OK
8. yellow
9. OK
10. yourself

page 5
2 consonants:
yes
yet
your
year
you're
3 consonants:
young
yard
4 or more consonants:
yellow
yourself
1 consonant:
you

page 6
1. city
2. any
3. very
4. pretty
5. happy
6. every
7. only
8. story
9. study
10. many

page 8
1. by, 1, by
2. my, 5, dry

3. try, 9, fly
4. fry, 4, fry
5. dry, 2, my
6. fly, 3, reply
7. sky, 7, sky
8. why, 10, supply
9. reply, 6, try
10. supply, 8, why

page 9
more than 3 letters:
reply & supply

page 10
"d" column
1. No
2. No
3. No
4. caked
5. raked
6. baked
7. braked
8. faked
9. No
10. No
"s" column
1. makes
2. takes
3. lakes
4. cakes
5. rakes
6. bakes
7. brakes
8. fakes
9. sakes
10. shakes

page 12
1. OK   6. came
2. game   7. OK
3. name   8. OK
4. OK   9. flame
5. OK   10. became

page 14
circled words:
1. insied
2. bried
3. besside
4. wied
5. deside
6. teid
7. seid
8. ried
9. ootside
10. hyde

page 15
1. ride; c2, v2
2. wide; c2, v2
3. tide; c2, v2
4. hide; c2, v2
5. bride; c3, v2
6. side; c2, v2
7. inside; c3, v3
8. outside; c3, v4
9. beside; c3, v3
10. decide; c3, v3
11. outside

page 16
1. spoke
2. stroke
3. choke
4. stoke
5. broke
6. woke
7. smoke
8. joke
9. poke
10. awoke

page 18
1. way, 10, always
2. day, 3, away

3. may, 5, day
4. say, 8, lay
5. stay, 9, may
6. lay, 4, pay
7. pay, 6, play
8. play, 7, say
9. away, 2, stay
10. always, 1, way

page 20
1. OK   6. OK
2. explain 7. gain
3. OK   8. contain
4. main   9. chain
5. OK   10. OK

page 23
longest word: detail

page 26
1. keep; c2, v2
2. deep; c2, v2
3. sleep; c3, v2
4. asleep; c3, v3
5. jeep; c2, v2
6. weep; c2, v2
7. beep; c2, v2
8. sheep; c3, v2
9. sweep; c3, v2
10. steep; c3, v2
11. asleep

page 28
beans—jeans
please—tease
real—deal
easy—queasy
clean—mean
speaks—leaks
sea—pea
team—cream
east—least

Answer Key (cont.)

page 29

longest words: please, speaks

page 30

1. eat, 3, beat
2. beat, 1, cheat
3. heat, 4, eat
4. meat, 5, heat
5. seat, 8, meat
6. neat, 6, neat
7. treat, 9, repeat
8. cheat, 2, seat
9. wheat, 10, treat
10. repeat, 7, wheat

page 31

longest word: repeat

page 34

1. continue
2. ruin
3. due
4. blue
5. fruit
6. value
7. true
8. suit
9. clue
10. argue

page 35

1. fruit; c3, v2
2. suit; c2, v2
3. ruin; c2, v2
4. due; c1, v2
5. blue; c2, v2
6. true; c2, v2
7. clue; c2, v2
8. argue; c2, v3
9. value; c2, v3
10. continue; c4, v4
11. continue

page 36

Lines drawn to make these pairs:

1. yarn——barn
2. hard——card
3. arm——farm
4. mark——dark
5. start——smart
6. car——far
7. large——barge
8. party

page 37

Answers will vary based on dictionary used.

page 39

2 consonants:

   her   over   ever

3 consonants:

   water

   never

   after

   paper

   under

4 consonants:

   person

   number

page 40

circled words:

1. mor
2. docter
3. fore
4. hoers
5. conr
6. foorm
7. boern
8. befor
9. shart
10. storie

page 41

1. for, 367
2. more, 6673
3. short, 74678
4. form, 3676
5. story, 78679
6. horse, 46773
7. born, 2676
8. corn, 2676
9. before, 233673
10. doctor, 362867
11. born & corn

page 42

1. return
2. OK
3. circle
4. OK
5. OK
6. OK
7. sir
8. bird
9. direct
10. OK

page 44

1. a
2. b
3. c
4. b
5. a
6. c
7. c
8. b
9. a
10. a
11. c
12. b
13. a
14. b
15. a

page 45

1. c
2. b
3. c
4. a
5. c
6. b
7. b
8. c
9. a
10. a
11. b
12. c
13. b
14. b
15. a

page 46

1. a
2. a
3. c
4. b
5. a
6. c
7. b
8. a
9. b
10. c
11. b
12. c
13. a
14. c
15. c
16. b
17. a
18. c
19. c
20. b

48

Teacher Created Materials

"Created *by* Teachers *for* Teachers"

Quality Resource Books
language arts
social studies
math
science
technology
the arts

Full Color Products
bulletin boards
border trim
stickers
awards
notepads
postcards
name tags
name plates
incentive charts
two-sided decorations

Educational Software
Professional Development

ISBN 0-7439-3772-4

50499

9 780743 937726

Teacher Created Materials, Inc.

PRINTED IN U.S.A.

ISBN 0-7439-3772-